ESSENTIAL ELEMENTS® RECORDER
CLASSROOM METHOD

W9-BMW-845

KAYE CLEMENTS   **PAUL LAVENDER**   **CHARLES MENGHINI**

Recorders are a part of the flute family and have been played for hundreds of years. Recorder-like instruments have been used in many different cultures and types of music – from accompanying dancing and singing, to performing concert music.

Recorders come in several sizes. The smaller they are, the higher they sound, and the larger they are, the lower they sound. In a school music program you will probably play the soprano recorder, one of the smaller instruments. The recorder may be played as a solo instrument (one featured player), or as a part of an ensemble (many players together).

Playing the recorder is an excellent way to learn the "essentials" of music, which can also prepare you to perform in other musical groups such as choir, band or orchestra.

With *Essential Elements® Recorder*, you will enjoy making music with your friends and classmates. Have fun!

ABOUT THE RECORDER

ISBN 1-4234-8127-5
Copyright © 2010 by HAL LEONARD CORPORATION
International Copyright Secured   All Rights Reserved

HAL•LEONARD® CORPORATION
7777 W. BLUEMOUND RD. P.O. BOX 13819 MILWAUKEE, WI 53213

GETTING STARTED

Assembling Your Recorder

- Recorders are made in one solid piece or three separate pieces.
- If your recorder is in three pieces, put it together to look like the picture.

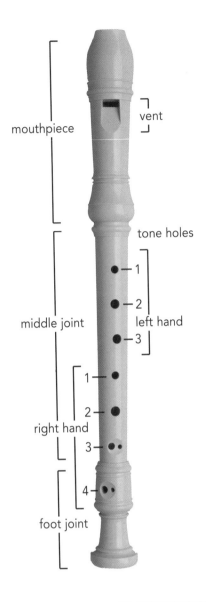

mouthpiece

vent

tone holes

1

2

left hand

middle joint

3

1

2

right hand

3

4

foot joint

Breathing and Air Flow

Your breath creates the "air stream" which allows the recorder to make its sound. The air stream should flow slowly and steadily.

Try this:

- Place the palm of your hand in front of your mouth.
- Pretend to take a "drink" of air, filling your belly.
- Keep your jaw relaxed, and shape your lips to let the air out slowly and steadily against your palm – like blowing soup in a spoon to cool it down. Be sure to blow gently, not hard.
- Repeat, but this time, pretend to say "doo(d)." Keep a steady flow of air to hold out the "oo" sound and make the final (d) silent to stop the air.

Your First Tone

A tone is a musical sound. The natural tone of the recorder is sweet and clear – not shrill or harsh.

To play your first tone:

- Hold the recorder upright with your left hand just below the vent opening on the mouthpiece. The vent should face away from you. Keep your chin level and relax your shoulders.
- Put the tip of the mouthpiece between your lips slightly in front of your teeth. Again, relax your jaw, "drink in" your air, and pretend to say "doo(d)." Hold out the "oo" sound and end with a silent (d).
- Make sure to blow gently without puffing your cheeks.

Practice the exercise below:

Care and Cleaning

- Use a cleaning rod to run a soft cloth through your recorder and gently into the mouthpiece. If your recorder has sections, take it apart to clean each part.
- Once in a while, you may want to clean your plastic recorder (not wood) in warm, soapy water and then rinse it in clear water. Let it dry before playing again.

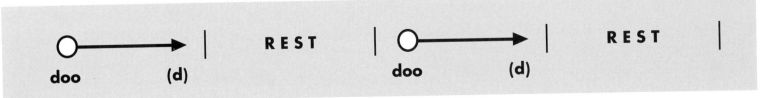

doo   (d)   REST   doo   (d)   REST

Placing Your Fingers

To play the recorder, the fingers of your left and right hands are numbered. (See pictures).

- Relax both hands and "stack" them so the left hand is on top.

- Hold the recorder with your right hand, with the mouthpiece up. Cover the hole on the back with your left thumb (LT).

- Cover the top three holes on the front with the 1st, 2nd and 3rd fingers of your left hand. Your left 4th finger (baby finger) does not cover a hole.

- Let your right thumb (RT) rest on the back, halfway between your left thumb (LT) and the bottom of the recorder.

- Cover the remaining holes on the front with the 1st, 2nd, 3rd and 4th fingers of your right hand.

- Compare your hand position with the pictures.

READING MUSIC

By reading music, you can learn to sing or play a song without hearing it first – just like reading a story.

Music Staff

The **music staff** has 5 lines and 4 spaces where notes and rests are written.

Ledger Lines

Ledger lines extend the music staff. Notes on ledger lines can be above or below the staff.

Measures & Bar Lines

Measure *Measure*

Bar line *Bar line* *Double bar line*

Bar lines divide the music staff into **measures**.

Double bar line indicates the end of a piece of music.

Treble Clef (G Clef)

indicates the position of note names on a music staff.

Time Signature

indicates how many beats per measure and what kind of note gets one beat.

= **4 beats** per measure

= **Quarter** note gets one beat

Note Names

Each note is on a line or space of the staff. These note names are indicated by the treble clef.

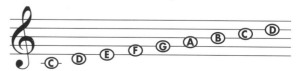

LET'S PLAY MUSIC

Quarter Note ♩ or ♩ = One Beat   **Quarter Rest** 𝄽 = One Silent Beat

Tonguing   The tongue starts the sound by releasing the air stream. Each tone should start with a soft "doo" sound. For notes followed by a rest, stop the air stream with a gentle, silent "d."

1. LET'S PLAY B

◁ To play "B," place your left thumb (LT) and first finger (L1) as shown. Your right thumb should rest on the back.

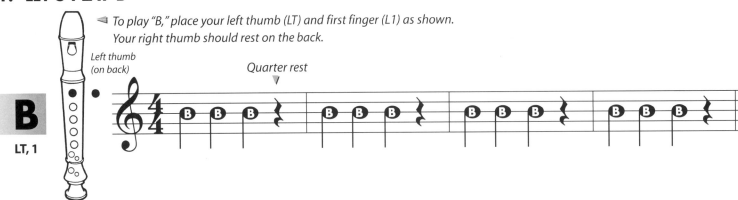

2. LET'S PLAY A

◁ To play "A," use your left thumb (LT) and two fingers (L1, 2).

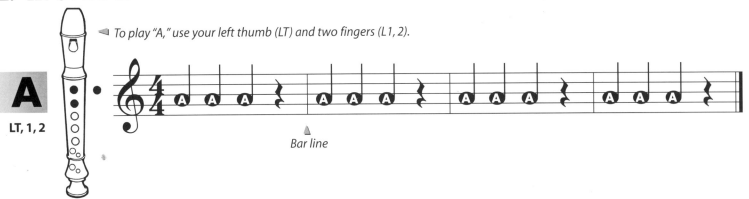

3. LET'S PLAY G

◁ To play "G," use your left thumb (LT) and three fingers (L1, 2, 3).

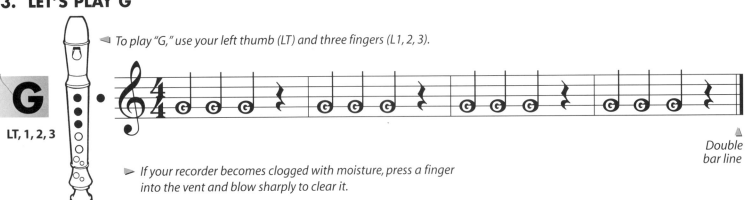

➤ If your recorder becomes clogged with moisture, press a finger into the vent and blow sharply to clear it.

REVIEW
Identify the notes (by letter name) and the symbols below. Write your answers on the blank lines.

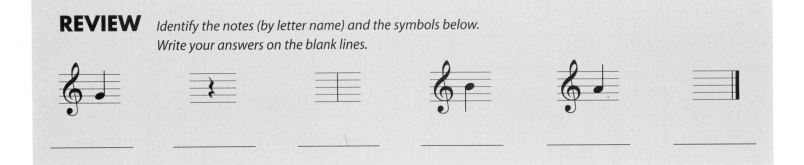

Tone

A tone is musical sound. To play a clear and sweet tone:

- Relax your jaw
- "Drink in" your air

- Use your tongue (doo) to gently release a steady air stream
- Blow gently, not hard

4. CHANGING NOTES

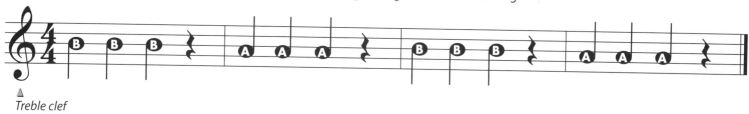

Lift your L3 finger during this rest.

Put your L3 finger down during this rest.

5. FROM THE TOP *Try to change to the next fingering during the rests in this song.*

Treble clef

6. UP AND DOWN *How many measures does this song have?*

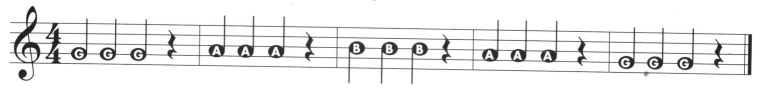

Rhythm

Rhythm is a pattern of notes and rests played over a steady beat.
No. 7 – *Watch The Rests* has a new rhythm.

7. WATCH THE RESTS

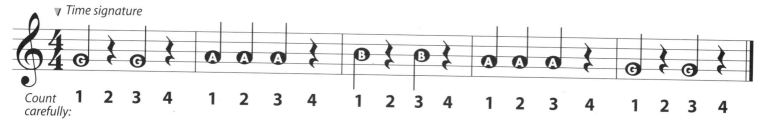

Time signature

Count carefully: 1 2 3 4   1 2 3 4   1 2 3 4   1 2 3 4   1 2 3 4

8. ESSENTIAL ELEMENTS QUIZ *Write in the counts below the notes and rests.*

9. NOTE CHECK   *Write in the remaining note names before playing.*

B   A _ _ _   _ _ _   _ _ _   _ _ _   _ _ _

△ *Write*

10. STEP IT UP   *Write in the note names.*

_ _ _   _ _ _   _ _ _   _ _ _   _ _ _   _ _ _

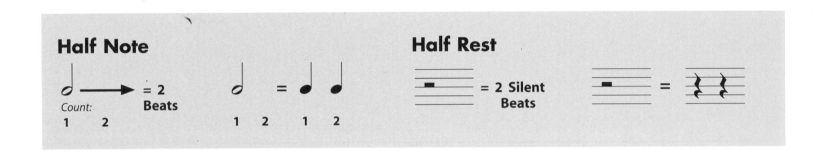

Half Note   ♩ → = 2 **Beats**   *Count:* 1 2

♩ = ♩ ♩   1 2 1 2

Half Rest   ▬ = 2 **Silent Beats**   ▬ = 𝄽 𝄽

11. STICK TOGETHER   *The note patterns in No. 10 and No. 11 are the same. How is the rhythm different?*

▽ *Half note*

1 2   1 2   1 2

12. TIME OUT

▽ *Half rest (2 beats)*

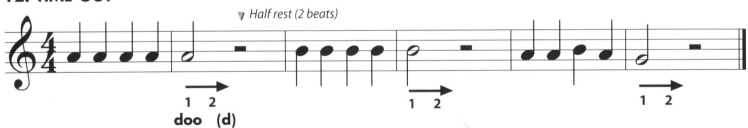

1 2   1 2   1 2

doo   (d)

Breath Mark   **,**   Take a quick, deep breath at the end of the note.
Be sure to play the next note on time.

---

13. HEADS UP

▽ *Breathe*   ▽ *Breathe*

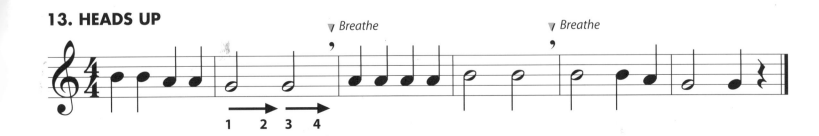

1   2   3   4

Melody

A melody is a combination of different notes and rhythms that makes a tune you can sing or play. *Happy Birthday* is a melody most people know. Can you think of other melodies?

14. WHAT'S BAKING? *Can you identify this familiar melody?*

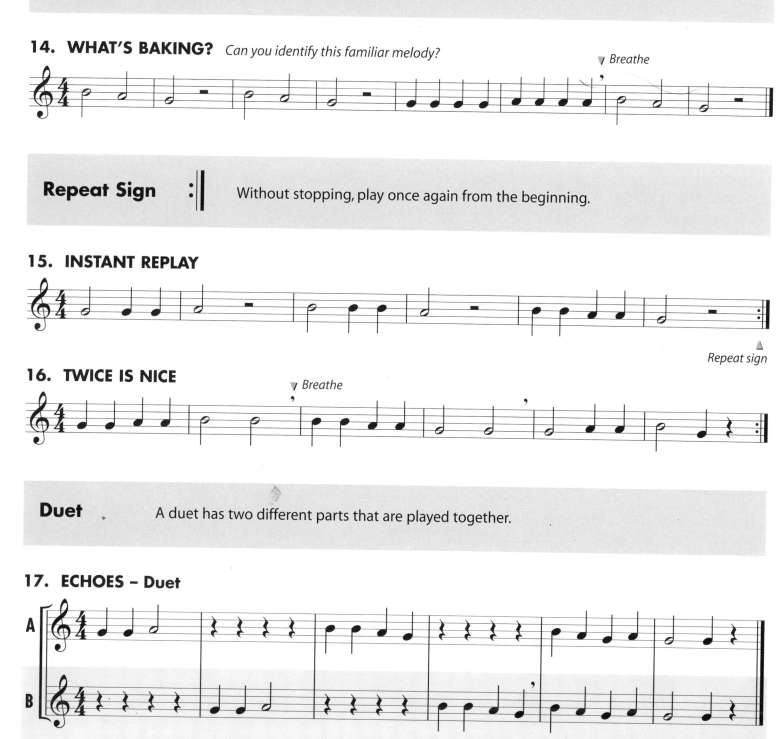

Repeat Sign :|

Without stopping, play once again from the beginning.

15. INSTANT REPLAY

16. TWICE IS NICE

Duet

A duet has two different parts that are played together.

17. ECHOES – Duet

18. ESSENTIAL CREATIVITY (Title)

Create your own title and words to fit the melody of this song.

Words ▶

8

19. AT PIERRE'S DOOR

French

Fermata 𝄐 Hold the note (or rest) longer than normal.

20. SKIPPING AROUND

Fermata

World Music People throughout the world have music that reflects their cultures. Sharing each other's music is a way of learning and connecting. *Suo Gan* is a lullaby from Wales, a country west of England in Great Britain. Welsh is the traditional language of Wales.

21. SUO GAN

Welsh

22. ROLLING ALONG

Traditional

Mer - ri - ly we roll a - long, roll a - long, roll a - long.

Mer - ri - ly we roll a - long, o'er the deep blue sea.

Eighth Notes

Each eighth note = ½ Beat
2 eighth notes = 1 Beat

1 ⌐

1 ⌐ 2 ⌐

Two or more eighth notes have a *beam* across the stems.

▼ *Beam*

=

When counting eighth notes, it helps to put the word "and" (⌐) between each main beat.

23. RHYTHM RAP

Clap:

$\frac{4}{4}$

Count: 1 2 3 4 1 2 3 ⌐ 4 1 2 3 ⌐ 4 1 2 3 ⌐ 4

24. EIGHTH NOTE GROOVE

Count: 1 2 3 4 1 2 3 ⌐ 4 1 2 3 ⌐ 4 1 2 3 ⌐ 4

25. RHYTHM RAP

Clap:

$\frac{4}{4}$

Count: 1 2 3 4 1 ⌐ 2 ⌐ 3 4 1 ⌐ 2 ⌐ 3 4

1 ⌐ 2 ⌐ 3 4 1 ⌐ 2 3 ⌐ 4 1 ⌐ 2 ⌐ 3 4

26. MIX 'EM UP *Write in the remaining counts before playing.*

1 2 3 4 1 ⌐

27. ESSENTIAL ELEMENTS QUIZ – HOP OLD SQUIRREL *This is your first playing quiz.*

Virginia

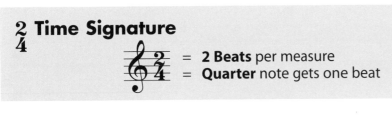

Time Signature

$\frac{2}{4}$ = **2 Beats** per measure

= **Quarter** note gets one beat

Conducting

Practice conducting this two-beat pattern.

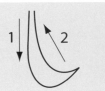

28. RHYTHM RAP

Clap:

Count: 1 2 1 2 1 ɇ 2 ɇ 1 2 ɇ 1 2 ɇ 1 ɇ 2 1 ɇ 2 ɇ 1 2

29. TWO BY TWO

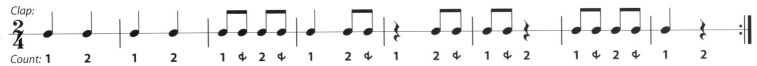

30. HOT CROSS BUNS

English

Hot cross buns! Hot cross buns! One a pen-ny, Two a pen-ny, Hot cross buns!

Tempo Markings

Tempo is the speed of music. Tempo markings are usually written in Italian above the staff.
Allegro – Fast tempo   **Moderato** – Medium tempo   **Andante** – Slower, walking tempo

31. THE BELL TOWER

Traditional

Andante

32. DOWN BY THE STATION

Traditional

Moderato

Down by the sta - tion, ear - ly in the morn - ing, See the lit - tle smoke puffs,

all in a row.   See the en - gine driv - er,   Toot! Toot! Off they go!

33. ON THE MARCH

Allegro ◁ *Fast tempo – continue to blow gently.*

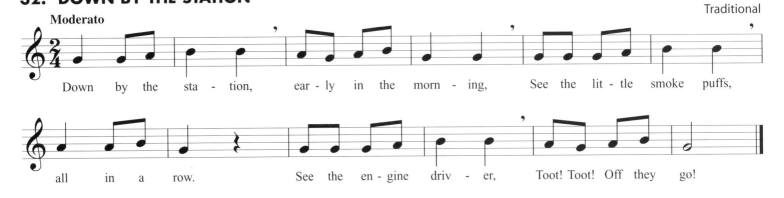

34. GOOD NEWS

Moderato — African-American Spiritual

Good news! Char-iot's a - com - ing! Good news! Char-iot's a - com - ing! Good news!

Char-iot's a - com - ing! Don't leave me be - hind! Don't you leave me here be - hind.

Pick-Up Notes

One or more notes that come before the first full measure are called **pick-up notes**. The beats of pick-up notes are subtracted from the last measure.

35. DRY BONES

Moderato — African-American Spiritual

△ *Pick-up*

Harmony

The sound of two or more notes played together is called **harmony**.

36. GRANDMA GRUNTS – Duet

Moderato — *Harmony* — Appalachian

37. ESSENTIAL ELEMENTS QUIZ – THE BOATMAN *(Playing Quiz)*

Allegro — Traditional

Where is beat 4? ▽

38. LET'S PLAY E – New Note

E is a low, soft note. Be sure to blow very gently and steadily. To play E, you will use both hands. When you lift fingers, keep them just above the holes they cover.

39. STAR LIGHT, STAR BRIGHT

Traditional

40. TRIBAL DANCE

41. FLOWER SONG

Dynamics

f – *forte* (loud) *mf* – *mezzo forte* (moderately loud) *p* – *piano* (soft)

Dynamics make music more interesting for the listener. Recorder groups can best perform dynamics by adding and subtracting players.

42. DING DONG DELL

Traditional

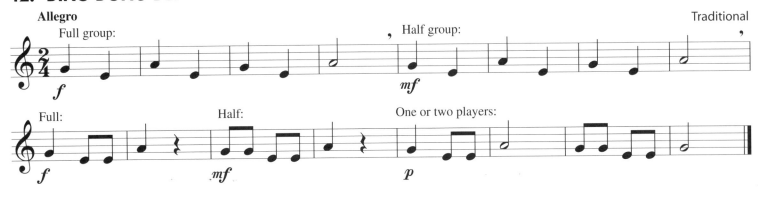

43. LUCY LOCKET

44. WONDERINGS *Is this in a fast or slow tempo?*

45. LITTLE SALLY WATER

46. A TISKET A TASKET

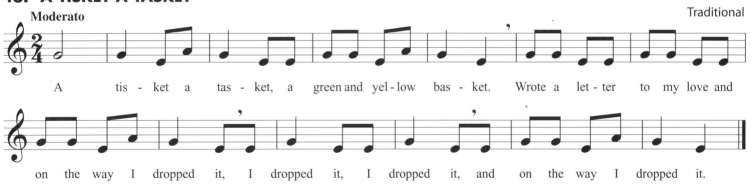

A tis-ket a tas-ket, a green and yel-low bas-ket. Wrote a let-ter to my love and

on the way I dropped it, I dropped it, I dropped it, and on the way I dropped it.

Composition

A composition is an original piece of music. A person who writes music is called a composer.

For No. 47, *Enchanted Melody,* compose and write down your own ending using the notes B, A, G, or E. Be sure to include 4 beats of music in each measure.

47. ESSENTIAL CREATIVITY – ENCHANTED MELODY

△ *Write*

Tie

A tie is a curved line connecting notes on the same line or space. Play one note for the combined counts of the tied notes.

1 Beat + 1 Beat = 2 Beats

48. FIT TO BE TIED

Moderato

△ *2 beats*

49. ALOUETTE

French-Canadian

Moderato

△ *3 beats*

Dotted Half Note

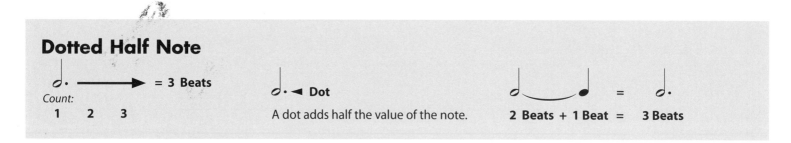

= 3 Beats

Count: **1 2 3**

Dot

A dot adds half the value of the note.

2 Beats + 1 Beat = 3 Beats

50. ALOUETTE – THE SEQUEL *Compare this to No. 49.*

French-Canadian

Moderato

51. KINGS AND CASTLES *Write in the remaining counts before playing.*

Moderato

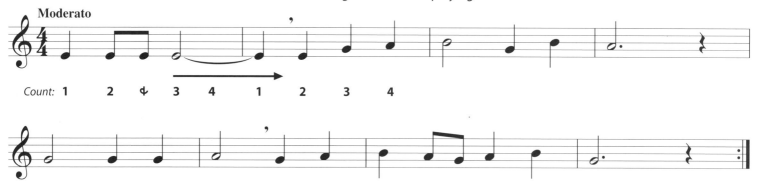

Count: **1 2 ȼ 3 4 1 2 3 4**

52. COUNTRY JIG

Allegro

3/4 Time Signature

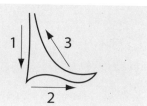

= **3 Beats** per measure
= **Quarter** note gets one beat

Conducting

Practice conducting this three-beat pattern.

53. RHYTHM RAP

54. THREE BEAT JAM

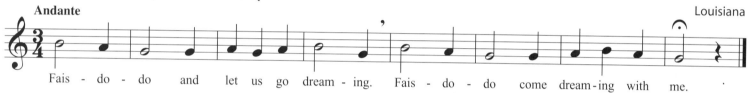

55. FAIS-DO-DO (FAY-doe-doe)

Fais - do - do and let us go dream - ing. Fais - do - do come dream-ing with me.

D.C. al Fine

At **D.C. al Fine,** play again from the beginning, stopping at **Fine** *(FEE- nay)*. **D.C.** is the abbreviation for **Da Capo**, which means "to the beginning," and **Fine** means "the end."

56. COURT DANCE

1st time, continue ▲

D.C. al Fine

▲
Go to beginning and play to Fine.

57. ESSENTIAL ELEMENTS QUIZ – ROCKIN' RESTS

58. LET'S PLAY D – New Note

*The note D is written in the space below the E line. Tongue softly with a gentle, steady air stream. Make sure R3 covers **both** holes.*

59. WALTZ PETITE

60. CHIPPEWA LULLABY

Phrase A phrase is a musical "thought" that is often 2 or 4 measures long. Try to play a phrase in one breath.

61. ONE, TWO, THREE, O'LEARY

62. HEY, BETTY MARTIN *Mark the phrases (ϑ) before playing.*

17

63. CHICKALILEELO

Moderato

Southern American

La la la chick-a-li-lee-lo, La la la chick-a-li-lee-lo,

I'm gon-na mar-ry who I please, La la la chick-a-li-lee-lo.

64. THE JOLLY MILLER

Allegro

Traditional

1st and 2nd Endings

Play through the 1st Ending. Then play the repeated section of music, *skipping* the 1st Ending and playing the 2nd Ending.

65. JOLLY OLD SAINT NICK

Moderato

Traditional

2nd time →

66. WAYFARING STRANGER

Andante   Full group:

Traditional

67. ESSENTIAL ELEMENTS QUIZ – OLD BRASS BAND

Moderato

Ozark Mountains

68. OLD MAC'S FARM

Moderato

Traditional

Repeat before continuing ▵

(1   2   3   4)

69. THE GREAT WALL *Mark the phrases (ˌ) before playing.*

Moderato

Fine

D.C. al Fine

70. HOLE IN THE BUCKET

Allegro

German

Where's beat 3? ▵

71. JOIN THAT BAND – Duet *Can you hear the melody move between part A and B?*

Allegro

Full group:

African-American Spiritual

▾ *Harmony*

A

B

▴ *2 beats*

A

B

72. LET'S PLAY C – New Note
Remember to keep your right hand fingers "floating" over their holes.

73. STEPPING OUT

> **Baroque Music**
>
> Music from the Baroque *(bah-ROKE)* Period (1600–1750) is known for its large choruses, string orchestras, pipe organs, and courtly dances. Bach, Vivaldi, and Handel were important Baroque composers. Handel's *Hallelujah Chorus* is a famous piece of Baroque music.

74. HALLELUJAH CHORUS

George Frideric Handel

75. VOLGA BOATMAN

Russian

76. BARCAROLLE

Jacques Offenbach

77. SILVER MOON BOAT

Japanese

78. ESSENTIAL ELEMENTS QUIZ – CRUISIN' THOSE Cs

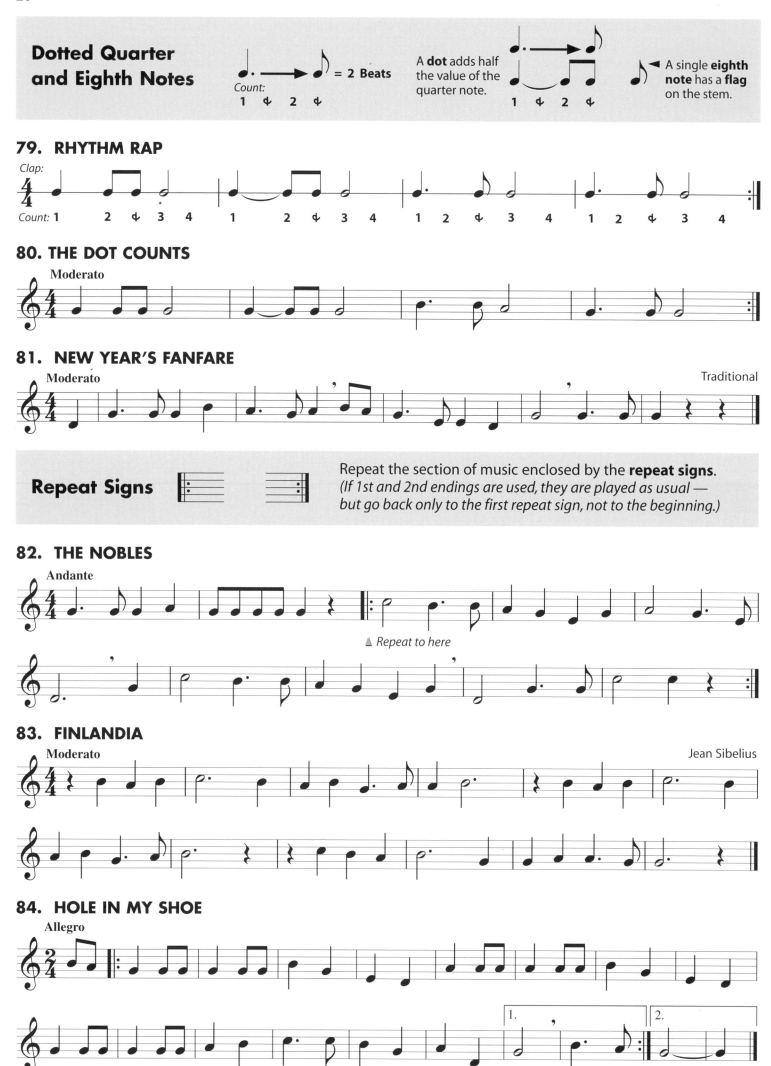

85. LET'S PLAY HIGH D – New Note
This note is played with one finger, L2. Keep your left thumb floating just over its hole. To keep your recorder steady, push gently with your right thumb.

86. AZTEC CHANT

87. TURNABOUT

Symphony During the Classical (1750–1825) and Romantic (1825–1900) Periods, the **symphony** was considered "popular" music, developed by composers such as Haydn, Mozart, Beethoven, Dvořák, and Brahms. Symphonies are usually written for large orchestra, and have four separate sections called *movements*.

88. ODE TO JOY (Symphony No. 9) – Duet
Ludwig van Beethoven

89. GOING HOME ("New World" Symphony)
Antonín Dvořák

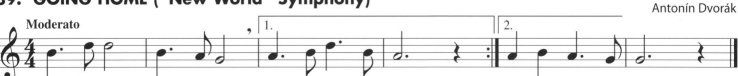

90. ESSENTIAL ELEMENTS QUIZ – GUTEN TAG!
German

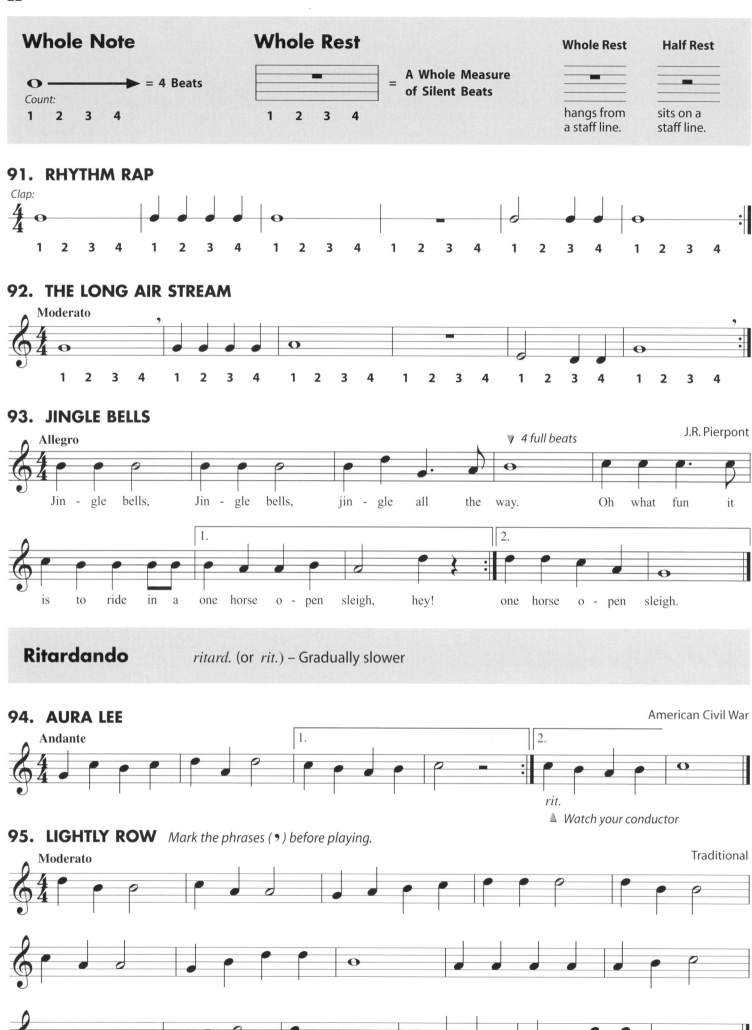

Whole Note

𝅝 ⟶ = 4 Beats

Count:
1   2   3   4

Whole Rest

▬ = A Whole Measure of Silent Beats

1   2   3   4

Whole Rest	Half Rest
hangs from a staff line.	sits on a staff line.

91. RHYTHM RAP

Clap:

1 2 3 4 | 1 2 3 4 | 1 2 3 4 | 1 2 3 4 | 1 2 3 4 | 1 2 3 4

92. THE LONG AIR STREAM

Moderato

1 2 3 4 | 1 2 3 4 | 1 2 3 4 | 1 2 3 4 | 1 2 3 4 | 1 2 3 4

93. JINGLE BELLS

J.R. Pierpont

Allegro

▼ *4 full beats*

Jin - gle bells,   Jin - gle bells,   jin - gle all   the   way.   Oh   what   fun   it

1. | *2.*

is   to ride in a   one horse o - pen sleigh,   hey!   one horse o - pen sleigh.

Ritardando

ritard. (or *rit.*) – Gradually slower

94. AURA LEE

American Civil War

Andante

1. | *2.*

rit.

▲ *Watch your conductor*

95. LIGHTLY ROW   *Mark the phrases (𝄐) before playing.*

Traditional

Moderato

rit.

96. JACK IN THE BOX *Can you identify this familiar melody?*

English

Staccato Staccato notes are played lightly and separated. They are marked with a dot above or below the note. Pretend to gently say "dut."

Legato Music marked *legato* is played smoothly and connected.

97. SHEPHERD'S HEY

English

98. CELTIC SEA

99. JESSE JAMES

Traditional

100. ESSENTIAL ELEMENTS QUIZ – WHEN THE SAINTS GO MARCHING IN

African-American Spiritual

△ *Count the rests*

101. LET'S PLAY F – New Note   *Make sure that R3 and 4 cover their holes completely.*

F

LT, 1, 2, 3
R 1, 3, 4

Moderato

△ F

△ *Be sure R4 is down*

American Music

Many cultures have influenced the music of the United States, including music brought to America by immigrants, and the music of Native Americans. The songs of composer Stephen Foster and "jazz" are examples of unique music styles developed in the United States.

102. CAMPTOWN RACES

Stephen Foster

Allegro

103. WHO'S THAT

Virginia

Moderato

Who's   that   tap-ping   at   my   win-dow?   Who's   that   knock-ing   at   my   door?

104. THE OX DRIVER

Kentucky

Andante

legato

105. THE MOCKING BIRD

Appalachian

Moderato

Full group:

f

One or two players:

p

Full group:

f

rit.

Sharp

A **sharp** raises a note to sound slightly higher and remains in effect for the entire measure. Notes without sharps are called **natural** notes.

106. LET'S PLAY F# (F-Sharp) – New Note

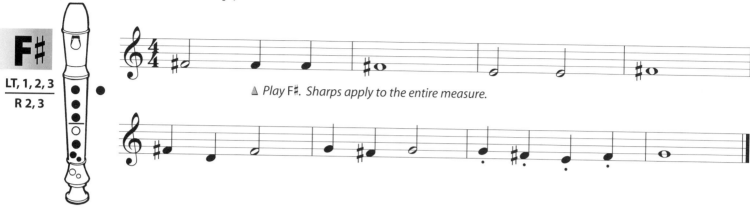

F#

LT, 1, 2, 3
R 2, 3

△ Play F#. Sharps apply to the entire measure.

107. ARE YOU SLEEPING – Round   *(When group A reaches ②, group B begins at ①)*

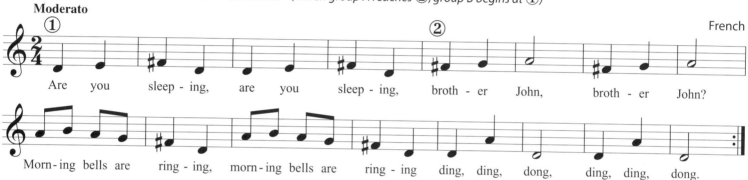

108. ROW, ROW, ROW YOUR BOAT – Round

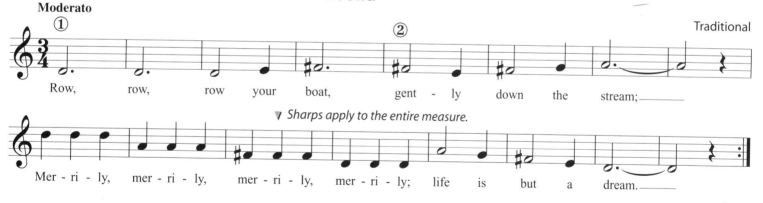

109. ASIAN DREAMS

110. ESSENTIAL ELEMENTS QUIZ – OH! SUSANNAH

111. BANANA BOAT SONG

Moderato   Fine   Jamaican

D.C. al Fine

112. SAILOR'S SONG

Allegro   Sea Chanty

Key Signature

This key signature indicates the key of G, which has all F-sharps. Play all F's as F-sharps.

113. TALLIS CANON – Round

Moderato   English

△ *G key signature – play all F's as F♯ (F-sharp)*

114. SHOO FLY

Allegro   Traditional

Shoo - fly, _____ don't both - er me, Shoo - fly, _____ don't both - er me.

Shoo - fly, _____ don't both - er me, I be - long to some - bod - y.

115. BINGO

Allegro   Traditional

△ *Always check the key signature before playing.*

1.

2.

Flat ♭

A **flat** lowers a note to sound slightly lower and remains in effect for the entire measure. Notes without flats (or sharps) are called **natural** notes.

116. LET'S PLAY B♭ (B-Flat) – New Note

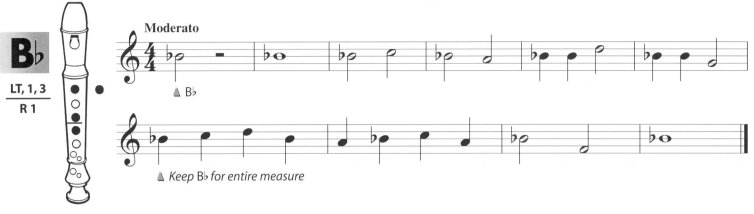

117. MARY ANN

Jamaican

₵ Time Signature

= **Common Time**
(Same as 4/4)

Conducting

Practice conducting this four-beat pattern.

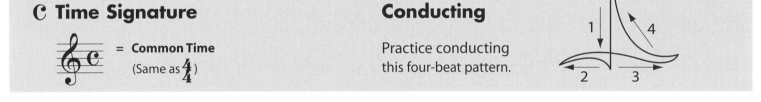

118. HEY HO! NOBODY HOME – Four-part Round

Traditional

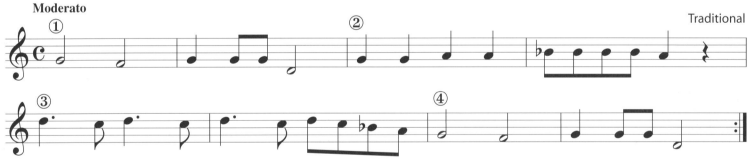

119. MICHAEL ROW THE BOAT ASHORE

African-American Spiritual

120. ESSENTIAL ELEMENTS QUIZ – FINALE FROM "NEW WORLD SYMPHONY"

Antonín Dvořák

121. LET'S PLAY LOW C – New Note
This C is the lowest note on the recorder. The left thumb and all fingers must cover all the holes. Blow very gently and tongue softly.

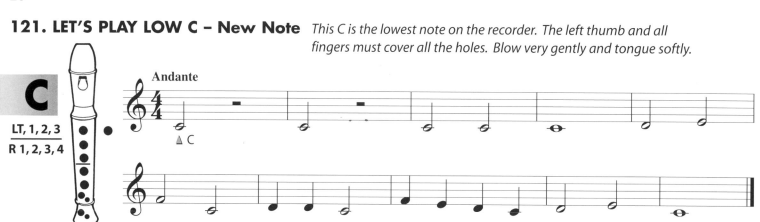

LT, 1, 2, 3 / R 1, 2, 3, 4

Andante

△ C

122. LONDON TOWNE – Round

English

Allegro

① ②

△ *Play B-natural (no flat indicated)*

123. CRIPPLE CREEK

Traditional

Allegro

New Key Signature

This key signature indicates the key of F, which has all B-flats. Play all B's as B-flats.

124. ALL THROUGH THE NIGHT

Traditional

Fine

Andante

△ *Play B♭'s throughout*

D.C. al Fine

Recorder Consort

During the Renaissance *(REHN-uh-sahnce)* Period (1400–1600), musicians often performed in recorder groups called "consorts." A consort includes four or more recorders of various sizes. The most common combination includes a soprano (your model), alto, tenor, and bass recorder.

125. ESSENTIAL ELEMENTS QUIZ – RENAISSANCE FAIRE

English

Allegro

Fine

D.C. al Fine

rit. (on D.C. only)

PERFORMANCE SPOTLIGHT

126. OLD JOE CLARK

Tennessee

127. SIMPLE GIFTS

Shaker

128. HATIKVAH

Israeli

129. UP ON THE HOUSETOP

Traditional

PERFORMANCE SPOTLIGHT

130. SCARBOROUGH FAIR

English

131. YANKEE DOODLE – Duet

Traditional

You can mark your progress through the book on this page. Fill in the stars as instructed by your teacher.

16

15

1

14

2

ESSENTIAL ELEMENTS®

13

3

STAR ACHIEVER

12

4

NAME _____

11

5

10

6

9

7

8

1. Page 2–3, Getting Started
2. Page 4, Review
3. Page 5, EE Quiz, No. 8
4. Page 7, Essential Creativity, No. 18
5. Page 9, EE Quiz, No. 27
6. Page 11, EE Quiz, No. 37
7. Page 13, Essential Creativity, No. 47
8. Page 15, EE Quiz, No. 57
9. Page 17, EE Quiz, No. 67
10. Page 19, EE Quiz, No. 78
11. Page 21, EE Quiz, No. 90
12. Page 23, EE Quiz, No. 100
13. Page 25, EE Quiz, No. 110
14. Page 27, EE Quiz, No. 120
15. Page 28, EE Quiz, No. 125
16. Page 29-30, Choose one song

MUSIC — AN ESSENTIAL ELEMENT OF LIFE

FINGERING CHART

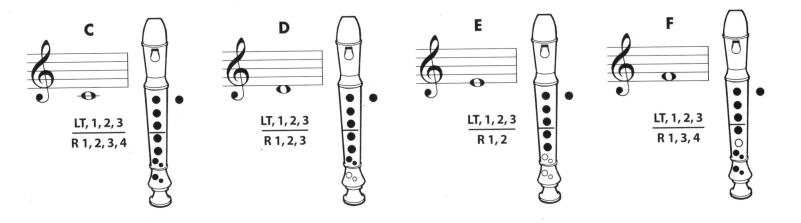

C

LT, 1, 2, 3
R 1, 2, 3, 4

D

LT, 1, 2, 3
R 1, 2, 3

E

LT, 1, 2, 3
R 1, 2

F

LT, 1, 2, 3
R 1, 3, 4

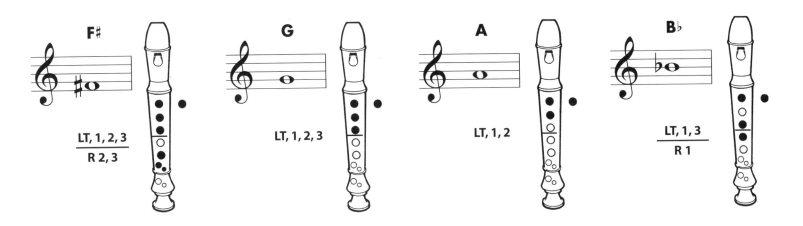

F#

LT, 1, 2, 3
R 2, 3

G

LT, 1, 2, 3

A

LT, 1, 2

B♭

LT, 1, 3
R 1

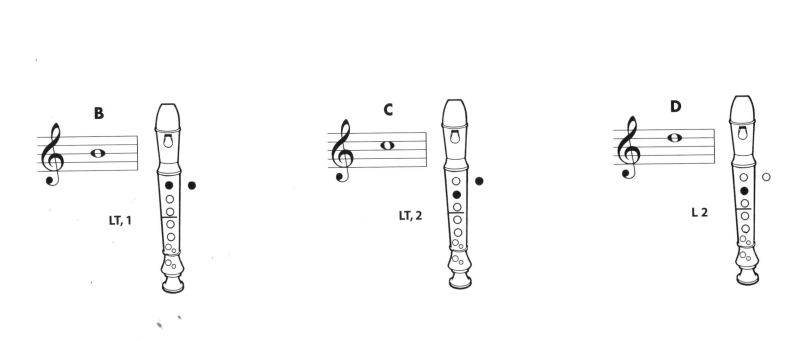

B

LT, 1

C

LT, 2

D

L 2